EMBSAY & BOLTON ABBEY STEAM RAILWAY

MIKE HEATH

HALSGROVE

First published in Great Britain in 2008

British Library Cataloguing-in-Publication Data
A CIP record for this title is available from the British Library

ISBN 978 1 84114 751 2

HALSGROVE
Halsgrove House
Ryelands Industrial Estate
Bagley Road, Wellington, Somerset TA21 9PZ
Tel: 01823 653777   Fax: 01823 216796
email: sales@halsgrove.com
website: www.halsgrove.com

Printed and bound by
Grafiche Flaminia, Italy

INTRODUCTION

T he Embsay & Bolton Abbey Steam Railway is a Preservation Society that operates steam trains over a 4.5 mile section of what was once a railway link between the Yorkshire towns of Skipton and Ilkley. The old market town of Skipton, the 'Gateway to the Dales' was rail connected in 1847 when the Leeds and Bradford (Shipley – Colne Extension) Railway built its line through Airdale to Skipton, extending to Colne a year later. In the nineteenth century the village of Ilkley had been transformed by the Victorians into a fashionable spa town thus creating the need for a rail connection that, courtesy of the Otley and Ilkley Joint Railway Company, duly arrived on 1 August 1865.

Whilst there were many plans to connect Skipton with Ilkley over subsequent years it was the Midland Railway that bridged the gap opening their rail link on 1 October 1888. The line was double tracked with intermediate stations at Embsay, Bolton Abbey and Addingham. One branch line was constructed from Embsay Junction to Grassington. During its lifetime in addition to the routine daily local passenger and freight services it was often used by trains diverted from the congested Aire Valley route. The early part of the twentieth century saw the introduction of paid leave and Bank Holidays. The 'priory' at Bolton Abbey had become a very popular tourist destination and special trains from the West Riding of Yorkshire and all over Lancashire arrived at Ilkley and Bolton Abbey stations bringing thousands of people to the area.

In the 1960s Doctor Beeching's railway cull extended to all lines in the locality with the exception of the Leeds – Ilkley line which was saved thanks to vigorous local opposition. The lines from Skipton to Grassington and Embsay also had stay of execution being retained for stone traffic from local quarries but the Ilkley to Embsay railway was closed in 1965 and all track lifted shortly after. Three years later the Grassington branch itself was under threat and local enthusiasts banded together forming the Embsay and Grassington Railway Preservation Society with the aim of saving a part of Yorkshire Dales' railway history by preserving the branch and operating trains for enthusiasts and tourists. Their initial aims were thwarted by Tilcon Ltd who took ownership of the local quarry and introduced a regular flow of stone trains along the route and a part of the branch is still operating today.

Undeterred the society turned its attention to the line from Embsay to Bolton Abbey adopting the Yorkshire Dales Railway Society as their official name. In the early seventies money was raised from footplate rides and passenger services run over the short stretch of line between Embsay and Embsay Junction, but in 1974 British Rail banned preservation groups from running trains on tracks leased from them citing insurance problems. Before trains could run again a Light Railway Order had to be obtained and it was May 1974 before all requirements were met. To avoid confusion as to the railway's location its name then changed to the 'Embsay Steam Railway' and once re-opened its volunteers set about extending the line towards Bolton Abbey. Through the efforts of the working members who raised funds and carried out much of the necessary work a one mile long extension to Skibeden was opened in 1982. In 1987 a further half mile had been completed to Holywell Halt where a new Station was built by the volunteers. Two miles from Embsay is Stoneacre Loop which was reached in April 1991 and was to be the extent of the journey for a number of years. The remaining track bed to Bolton Abbey and the station site itself was purchased by the mid 1990s. The station ruins were beyond restoration so a new building was constructed with help from Yorkshire Television's Action Time programme. Businesses supplied materials free, or heavily discounted, and Sir Robert McAlpine Ltd carried out construction work free of charge. Stoneacre Loop was relaid for through traffic and Bolton Abbey re-opened to passenger trains on the 26 October 1997.

Unlike most preserved railways where ex-industrial locomotives were used to start running steam train services then discarded and replaced by larger ex-British Railways engines, the Embsay & Bolton Abbey Steam Railway prides itself on its collection of ex-industrial tank engines and the fact that working examples operate all steam services.

The line passes for its entire length through a glorious undulating landscape of stonewalled fields with a scattering of villages nestling in the hillside. Not a retail park or industrial estate in sight.

My first visits were back in the early eighties as what became annual family outings to their spooky Halloween trains, the exciting Bonfire Nights, sadly no longer held, and of course the Santa Specials. Enthusiasts' events such as the 'Harvest of Steam' have since been added to my diary as have the 1940s Weekend and I have even been present at a couple of Thomas the Tank Engine extravaganzas!

The line has always been family-orientated but has also managed to cater well for the railway enthusiast.

It markets itself as Yorkshire's 'Friendly Line' a title that is thoroughly deserved as I hope this book will show.

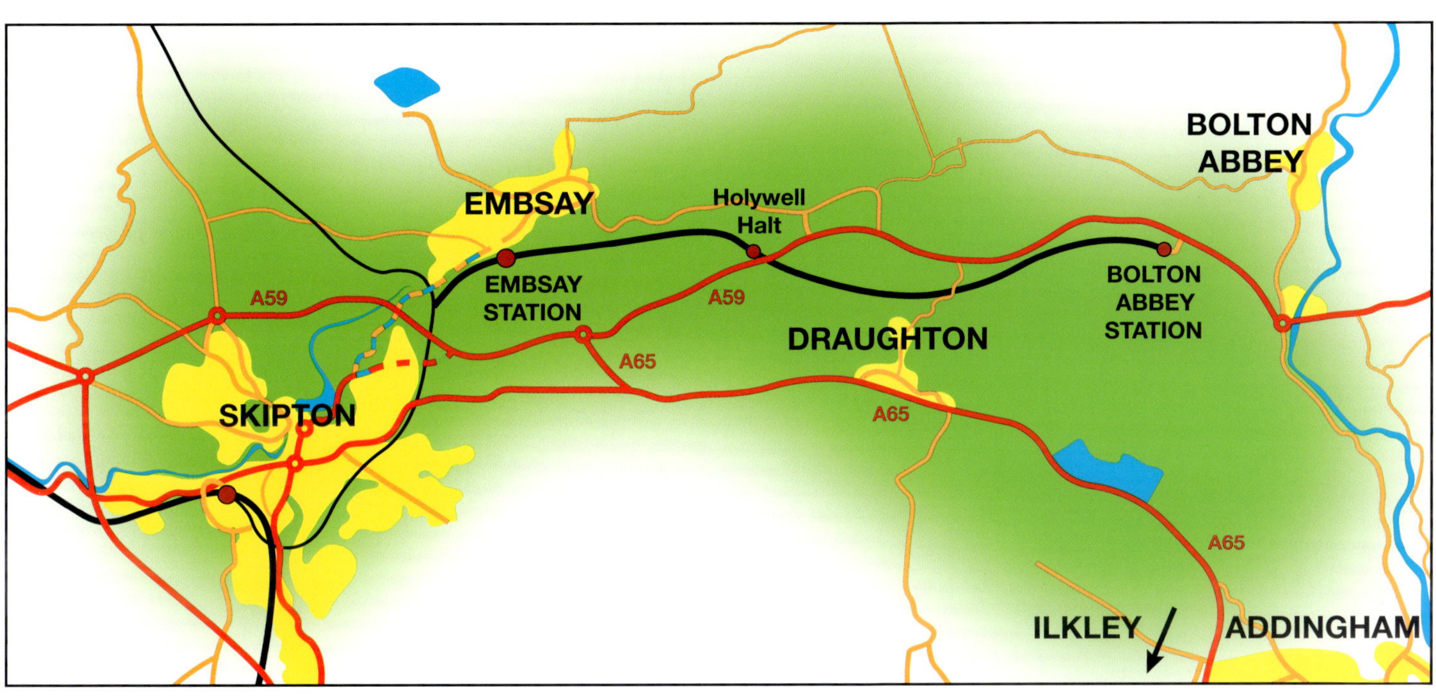

BOLTON ABBEY
EMBSAY
Holywell Halt
A59
EMBSAY STATION
A59
DRAUGHTON
BOLTON ABBEY STATION
SKIPTON
A65
A65
A65
ILKLEY
ADDINGHAM

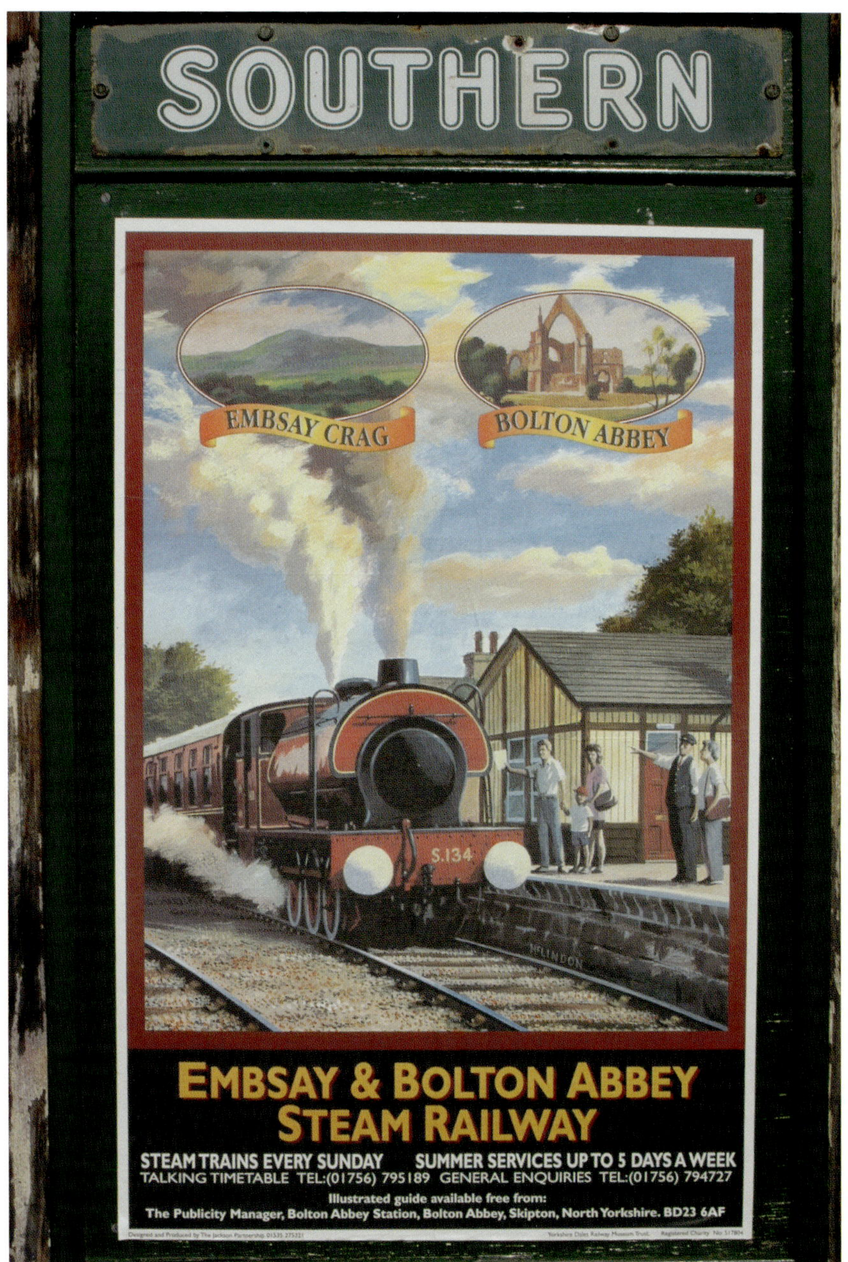

From the earliest days of railways, posters have adorned station notice boards extolling the virtues of tourist attractions and resorts all over the country. The tradition has continued into the preservation era with this colourful poster photographed at Havenstreet on the Isle of Wight Steam Railway.

One of my first visits to the railway was in September 1986 for that year's enthusiasts' event the 'Harvest of Steam'. There alongside the platform were two 0-6-0 Saddle Tank locomotives. 'Slough Estates No. 5' dating from 1939 when it was built, by Hudswell Clarke, for work on the Slough Trading Estate in Buckinghamshire where it spent all its working life until withdrawal in the mid 1970s. To the rear was 'Darfield No.1', built by Hunslet in 1953 for the National Coal Board's Darfield Main Colliery in Barnsley. It had arrived at Embsay in December 1975.

A few minutes later, under a very inclement sky, the pair were captured powering a passenger service back into Embsay Station having just run round their train at Bow Bridge near the former Embsay Junction.

Later in the day 'Darfield No.1' was piloted by another product of the Hunslet works, No. 7 'Beatrice'. This locomotive, built in 1945, arrived at Embsay in 1977 from the Ackton Hall Colliery, near Pontefract.

Completing the roster that weekend were 0-4-0ST No. 22, a 1952 product of Andrew Barclay's works in Kilmarnock and 0-6-0 ST S134 'Wheldale'. This was my introduction to both the railway and its varied collection of ex-industrial locomotives rousing an interest that has lasted to this day. (The bouncy castle was good too!)

Two years later in 1988 the railway celebrated the centenary of Embsay Station. For the event they hired in a locomotive that actually pre-dated the station. Built in 1874 for work at the Haydock Collieries in the heart of the Lancashire coalfield, the 0-6-0 Well Tank 'Bellerophon' represents a watershed in locomotive design. The Haydock Foundry had broken new ground with the first successful application of the piston valve and was also ahead of the game in fitting outside cylinders and motion. The 'Old Lady' prepares to depart Embsay for the run round loop at Bow Bridge with a Halloween special.

When the society obtained their Light Railway Order in 1979 they were then able to operate regular steam hauled passenger services between Embsay and Bow Bridge Junction with the eventual aim of extending towards Bolton Abbey in manageable stages as funds and labour permitted.

Having deposited its coaches in the loop, 'Bellerophon' prepares to run round the train in readiness for the return journey.

Well before Harry Potter's first lesson at Hogwarts School this Wizard faced locomotive conjured up a spectacular run past for those on the platform and footbridge at Embsay. 'Bellerophon' is also unique in being the only survivor of all six engines ever built by the Haydock Foundry and was saved from the cutter's torch in 1964 finding its way to the Keighley and Worth Valley Railway. In 1981 it was purchased by the Vintage Carriages Trust for the peppercorn price of £1 and restoration work commenced leading to a first steaming in preservation on 1 May 1985. At the time of writing a further period of restoration is nearing completion at the Foxfield Railway.

Between service trains the railway's shunting locomotives, both steam and diesel, can often be seen busying themselves in and out of the station. This ex-British Rail class 04 was built by Vulcan / Drewry, in 1952, for work on the Wisbech and Upwell Tramway in East Anglia where it would have been fitted with sideplates, covering the wheels and motion, and cowcatchers. 'Mavis' of Thomas the Tank Engine fame is thought to have been based on this locomotive.

'Ann' is a vertical-boilered Sentinel locomotive which was built in 1927 and is believed to be the oldest original example in existence. She spent all her working life at British Tar Products Limited at Irlam near Manchester.

The next two photographs highlight the changes in livery that railways often apply to locomotives after overhaul. Here, alongside the coaling stage 'No. 22' is in the red livery it would have carried when working at the East Hetton Colliery.

By 1994 the black livery of the Fishburn Coke Works had been applied. For the purists this was not a genuine change as whilst the locomotive had worked the Coke Works it had never been painted in this manner.

Opposite:
More activity alongside the platforms as S121 'Primrose No. 2' shunts
a vintage carriage in front of the station's main building.

In the yard on the coal dock by the water tower the fire has been lit to pressure test the recently restored boiler of 'Beatrice'. If successful it will be placed back in the frames and work will start in earnest on reassembling the locomotive.

Opposite:
Winter running provides the opportunity for some night photography.
No. 22 idles the evening away alongside the listed signalbox.

No 22
N. C. B.
EAST HETTON COLLIERY
50

Backlighting from the coal dock lamp has produced a dramatic silhouette and the time exposure has recorded the throwing out of the embers as a cascade of fire.

Here the glowing remnants of the fire have illuminated the wheels and motion of No. 68005.
The cover of dark and the coal dock lamp complete a timeless scene.

NCB
121

Halloween 1993 and No. 7 'Beatrice' has the right of way for the next night time departure which at that time would be to Stoneacre Loop.

Opposite:
S.121 'Primrose No. 2' is portrayed under similar circumstances.

A bit of infill flash has been used to highlight S.134 'Wheldale' just prior to departure.
The orange glow beyond the water tower confirms that this is a Bonfire Night special.

A small crowd of people have forsaken the warmth of the bonfire and gathered on the platform as 'Wheldale' puts on a 'sight and sound' show of its own before proceeding into the night.

Before moving off, footplate crews check the road ahead
is clear and that they have the signalman's permission
to pull away from the station.

Opposite:
Branch Line Day 1992 and the crew of 'Beatrice' keep
a watchful eye on the movements of No. 22 as they
await the right-away for their train.

BEATRICE
BEWARE OF TRAINS
No 2

The footbridge is a popular vantage point from where to watch, and photograph, the trains as they pull out of the station. It is also where those of a 'Werther's Original' age try to convince their children and/or grandchildren of the memories stirred by the delightful whiff of steam!

One sunny afternoon in the late nineties
I spent a good half hour taking a photograph
of this porter's trolley. The trolley itself was
no real problem but framing the two
locomotives between its cross rails, and the
footbridge notice within one of the hooped
metal feet did require some delicate
manoeuvring. A good photograph is all
down to composition and patience!

On summer Sundays between June and September there is an opportunity to travel first class in carriages from the historic 'Stately Trains' collection. These date from the Victorian era and have been lovingly restored to their original magnificence. (Karl Heath)

Spot the difference! Actually 'Beatrice' and 'Primrose No. 2' are both products of the Hunslet factory in Leeds and identical, save for the liveries and the stovepipe chimney fitted to the latter, which is also seven years younger being built in 1952. It had previously worked for the National Coal Board at their Peckfield Colliery, Micklefield.

One of those experimental photographs that are taken on a whim. In this case I had just arrived in the car park at Embsay and noticed that the steam from the locomotive was shading the light from the sun creating what I consider to a very atmospheric shot.

Spectacular departures are more or less guaranteed as the former industrial
workhorses get to grips with their new role hauling passenger trains.

1993 saw the first tender-engine hauling trains on the preserved railway. Former London Midland and Scottish Class 4F No. 4422 visited from the then North Staffordshire Railway (now known as the Churnet Valley Railway). It spent June – September on the line and here is seen hauling a demonstration freight train during the Steam Gala Weekend on the 12 September.

The pair of Hunslets seen earlier have received the 'right-away' and are blasting their way out of Embsay. In the distance beyond the crane is the original Midland Railway goods shed where for many years the preserved engines were serviced and maintained.

Diesel Weekend 2007. Note that a new much larger shed, under construction, now occupies the old goods yard. The society mindful of the need to provide covered accommodation for all its rolling stock had embarked on their 'Embsay Shed Project' back in the 1990s. Having raised money they constructed the foundations, purchased and erected the steelwork leaving the skeletal frame awaiting cladding. The opportunity to acquire Bolton Abbey Station and thus extend the railway meant that the shed project had to be put on the back burner. Despite disappointment at failing to secure a grant from the National Lottery in 2006 an application for European funding was successful allowing them to clad the entire structure. The old goods shed has been dismantled for eventual reconstruction at Bolton Abbey.

Wine and Dine specials have featured in the railway's programme of special services and this LNER carriage was rebuilt in preservation as a first class Restaurant Car for that very purpose. It actually started life in 1935 built as a general passenger vehicle and survived as one of the 'Control Trains' for use in times of emergency as a communications centre. It arrived at Embsay in the late 1970s.
The coach is now based on the North Yorkshire Moors Railway.

For the first mile out of Embsay the railway follows a perfectly straight path as far as the siding at Skibeden. The three car Diesel Multiple Unit is approaching the siding which from 1982 until 1987 was the terminus for services being the first stage of the railway's push towards Bolton Abbey.

To the south of the line is the former Skipton Rock Company's Haw Bank Quarry which has been worked for limestone since that company's incorporation in 1895. Now part of the Tilcon Quarry Products business the quarry is only used for the coating of limestone brought in by road from Tilcon's Swinden Quarry. The quarry used to have its own railway network with a link to the Skipton-Ilkley line at Embsay. Very little of this remains but the course can be traced in the carriage sidings at Embsay.

The sun shone for the 'Harvest of Steam' in 2002. 'Cranford' and 'Monckton No. 1' have just passed the siding at Skibeden and are now on the approach to Holywell Halt with a demonstration freight. The village of Embsay nestles on the hillside in the background.

Opposite:
At this point a public footpath crosses the line via a footbridge from where this photograph was taken.
(It is also where I first discovered that Hasselblad cameras do not bounce on concrete steps.)

Eastby Crags is a rocky outcrop above the village from where there is a panoramic view of the area.
Even from the road below the Crags the progress of a train can be followed for the entire
route from Embsay to Holywell Halt, whether on a hazy summer's day . . .

. . . or a chilly winter's afternoon.

The restored railway arrived at Holywell Halt in 1987. Twenty years later the Heritage Diesel Multiple Unit was photographed passing through. DMUs are very economical to operate, hence their introduction by British Rail to replace steam, and they certainly afford passengers all-round vision and the opportunity to share the driver's view of the route ahead.

Here the volunteers decided to construct a typical rural halt. Then, as now, there was only a single line running alongside the platform so after the passengers had disembarked the train would reverse to Skibeden Loop to run round and then push the coaches back to the halt. To satisfy light railway regulations the guard occupied a specially constructed compartment at the 'front' of the train. This was provided with an emergency brake which was used for the half mile between the loop and halt.

The halt is surrounded by a small wooded area which the society acquired and developed as a picnic and recreation site. Other than by request, trains rarely stop at the halt these days and as there is no other public access, this enchanting little glade is rarely used.

Just beyond the halt is Holywell Bridge which carries the busy A59 trunk road over the railway. Following closure of the line the local authority, on discovering that the bridge structure was deteriorating, planned to reinforce it by infilling the cutting below. This would have been a major obstacle to the preservation group's plans to extend the line. However, following a local campaign an alternative solution was agreed and with the co-operation of the North Yorkshire County Council and Craven District Council a steel tunnel method of reinforcement was introduced allowing sufficient clearance for a single line track to pass beneath.

Thus far the tracked had been purchased directly from British Rail or leased from Tilcon Ltd. The section beyond the A59 bridge had already been sold off by British Rail and had therefore to be repurchased at much more inflated prices. I wonder if the volunteers faced with that deteriorating bridge really believed that the railway would once again witness the splendid sight of an ex London Midland and Scottish Class 4F locomotive hauling an all maroon rake of coaches through the cutting, albeit in 1993.

The bridge seen in the background, which carries a farm track over the railway, is from where the previous photograph was taken. Peckett 0-4-0ST 'Annie' has just passed beneath it with a two coach working and is about to enter Stoneacre Loop.

Stoneacre Loop is just about the half-way point between Embsay and Bolton Abbey. This was the eastern end of the line between 1992 and 1997 and is now used as a passing loop when two trains are running. The signal box was built from scratch on the bog which surrounds this location!

Dry stone walls, rolling hills and meandering valleys typify the Yorkshire Dales landscape. The signal in
the centre locates Stoneacre Loop with the steam in the background showing the train is passing by Draughton.
This view from a public footpath that leads from the A59 above Holywell Halt.

In spring 2007 0-6-0ST 'Jessie' visited from the Llangollen Railway and has just passed beneath
Priors Lane Bridge which carries the road that links the village of Draughton with the
main A59 road seen top right. A seasonal carpet of bluebells covers the hillside.

Opposite:
For the next half mile the railway runs in a straight line parallel to the A59. Late in the day with the camera
shaded from the low direct sunlight, and an unusual break in traffic, I was able to take this glorious shot.

A few moments later and the train is about to enter Hambleton Cutting, a wooded, picturesque part of the line.

At the east end of the cutting the line opens out alongside the derelict Hambleton Quarry
and the footplate crew of No. 22 will be within sight of Bolton Abbey signal box and the station beyond.

In June 1998, shortly after the railway re-opened to Bolton Abbey, a Steam Gala was held with demonstration freights running between passenger services. On the final approach to the eastern terminus is visiting ex London and North Eastern Railway Class J27 0-6-0 mixed traffic tender locomotive No. 65894.

Later the same day No. 68005 is on freight duties. Despite the number and livery this is not an ex British Railways locomotive. It was built by Robert Stephenson & Hawthorn in 1945 for the National Coal Board and spent all its life in industrial service. It had been converted to resemble a BR version by the East Somerset Railway before finding itself transferred to Yorkshire in 1994.

Paired with 'Monckton No. 1', 68005 at the head of another freight working slows to stop alongside the platform at Bolton Abbey. Note the old coaches on the station forecourt.

Opposite:
Examples of vintage local road transport are often parked in the station forecourt adding to the period atmosphere and creating a scene seemingly untroubled by time.

BIBBY'S
PRIVATE
ACC 629
HUDDERSFIELD
BRADFORD
SKIPTON
LFM 767
TELEPHONE
L M S
KILLARNEY

The railway took ownership of the station site in 1993 but with a lot of hard work supported by grant aid from the European Regional Development Fund and English Partnerships and tremendous assistance from the railway and construction industries trains ran again between Embsay and Bolton Abbey four years later.

A completely new station was built, to a Midland Railway design, replacing the original derelict timber building which had to be removed due to its dangerous state. Sir Robert McAlpine & Co. Limited undertook construction work free of charge and many businesses supplied materials and equipment free or at heavily discounted prices. This beautifully restored station has rightly won several awards and was highly commended by the Heritage Railway Association.

Timber palisade fencing, platform lamp standards, porter's trolleys, weighing machines and the ever-present milk churns complete the country station ambience.

Not forgetting the countless hoardings enticing the traveller to venture further afield by visiting one of the many tourist attractions and holiday resorts that in the railway's heyday were all easily accessible by train.

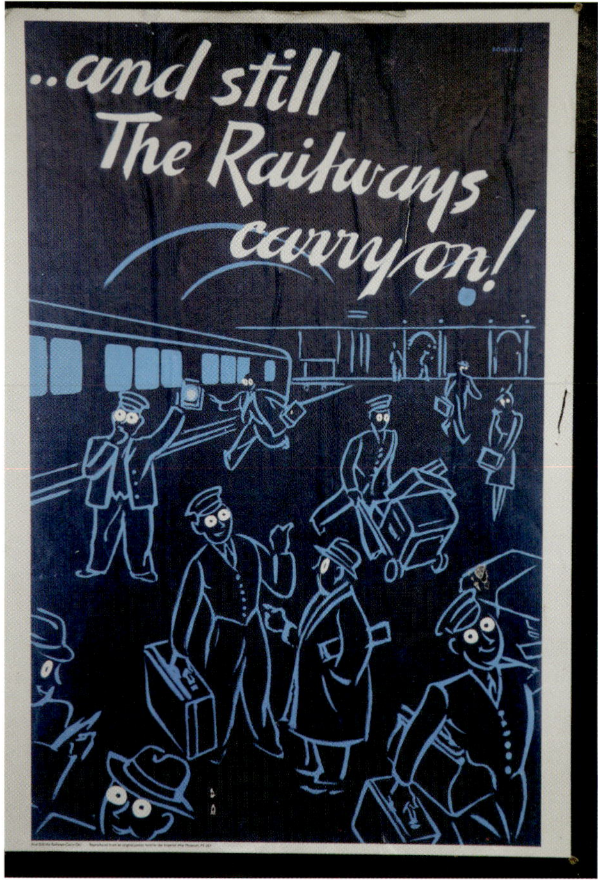

Over one weekend each year the railway takes on a 1940s' appearance as the role of the railways during the war years is affectionately commemorated.

A small military camp is set up in the station grounds.

64

Civilian and military re-enactors travel up and down the line giving the whole railway a wartime movie set appearance.

Period vehicles fill the station forecourts at both Embsay and Bolton Abbey.

'Brief Encounters' take place by the NAAFI!

As ever the cleaners eavesdrop the 'chat up lines' at the next compartment
and keep a beady eye on the spiv outside the waiting room!

The Home Guard are represented keeping the public informed but,
'Lest We Forget', a reminder of the serious consequences of war is not far away.

The extensive forecourt and large car park at Bolton Abbey allows the railway to host events for other preservation societies. Recent years have seen the White Rose Vehicle Rally take possession over two weekends in October with vintage cars, bikes, buses and wagons taking centre stage. (Karl Heath)

Embsay Station also plays host to vintage vehicles and this 1959-built 6 ton Scammel Scarab tractor and trailer, which used to work at the Cadbury Bourneville factory in Birmingham, is no stranger. When parked by the booking office within sight of the red phone box and telegraph pole standing by the station garden, a once common rural station scene is recreated.

The original railway reached Bolton Abbey in 1888 and special trains from all over the north of England brought visitors for a day out on the The Priory estate. Now the preserved railway provides a similar service and the walks by the River Wharf, through the surrounding woodland and into the village itself, are well worth a visit before returning to Embsay by train.

The signal box at Bolton Abbey is a Midland Railway 'box brought in from Guiseley and the water tower came from Skipton Station. 'Monckton No. 1' passes between the two whilst running round.

Saddletank 'Cranford No. 2' dates from 1942 and was built by Bagnall for use at the Cranford Ironstone Quarry in Northamptonshire. Standing alongside in the run round loop is the Sidetank locomotive No. 140. This was a 1948 product of the Hudswell Clarke factory and it worked at the National Coal Board's Horden Colliery in County Durham before coming to the railway.

Low December sun illuminates this double headed 'Special' preparing to transport excited passengers on a journey which will include a visit by Santa and an early Christmas present for the younger travellers.

Having 'hooked on' to the coaches in the station No. 68005 has steam
to spare as it prepares to commence the return journey.

For the 2007 Santa Special season the railway hired in, from the South Devon Railway, 0-6-0 Pannier Tank No. 1369. This particular locomotive had been built at Swindon in 1934 and spent a part of its working life shunting Waterloo Boat Trains on Weymouth Quay. Although in unfamiliar surroundings the little tank engine looked quite at home paired with the railway's own industrial locomotive.

A late afternoon return working heading back to Embsay viewed from alongside the signal box at the westerly end of the platform.

Opposite:
This and the next photograph were taken from the edge of the disused Hambleton Quarry over the Gala Weekend back in June 1998 when the weather played its part by providing superb lighting conditions.

The J27 Class of locomotive were designed for heavy freight work on the North Eastern Railway. This particular example was the last of the class to be built, in Darlington, in 1923. Much of its career was spent at York where following nationalisation in 1948 it was renumbered 65894. In 1966 it was transferred to Sunderland to work East Durham coal trains but was withdrawn from service in September the following year. On the 13 November 1967 it was purchased for preservation and following overhaul arrived at the North Yorkshire Moors Railway in October 1971.

Emerging from the wooded Hambleton Cutting on a return journey in July 2000
is diminutive 0-4-0 ST 'Annie' with a vintage 'Stately Trains' service.

The stretch of the A59 road that runs parallel to the railway includes a number of lay-bys allowing the photographer to park safely and provides a number of vantage points from which to photograph the passing trains.

From the fields on the other side of the railway, accessed from Priors Lane, a totally different landscape fills the frame. Again the bluebells add colour to the scene.

At this location, near to Priors Lane, the Midland Railway had propsed siting a station to serve Draughton. They carried out landscaping work but then abandoned the idea! This and the next photograph are of the same train and serve to highlight the difference between a steam in the landscape shot and the more traditional front three-quarter locomotive portrait.

Opposite:
In the winter months the landscape loses its colour but the cold air holds on to the steam which can hang above the line long after the train has passed.

This also highlights the benefits of having my son Karl accompany me on photographic expeditions. More often than not he seeks to find a different angle for the photograph and is almost always successful! (Karl Heath)

Working to the Santa Special timetable the Embsay-bound train approaches Priors Lane Bridge as, in the distance, that heading to Bolton Abbey is entering the loop at Stoneacre.

'Cranford No. 2' is approaching Priors Lane where the railway passes under a bridge which carries the road to Draughton.

Viewed from opposite the gated road entrance to the railway's yard at Draughton, the last train of the day pulls away from Stoneacre as the sun sets and the sky begins to colour up.

The summer of 2000 saw another visitor from the North Yorkshire Moors Railway working the line. Built in 1904, by Kitsons of Leeds, 0-6-0 No. 29 was employed in the north east at the Lambton Hetton and Joicey Collieries prior to preservation. On 16 July the Lambton tank was photographed waiting patiently in the loop at Stoneacre.

0-4-0 Saddle Tank locomotive 'Annie' was built by the Bristol-based Peckett and Sons, in 1908, for the Yates Duxbury Ltd's paper mills on the outskirts of Bury in East Lancashire. It was only withdrawn from active service in 1970 but became a victim of vandals and was in a sorry state when rescued from the cutter's torch, initially by the Bury Transport Museum until 1984 when it was purchased by a society member who fully overhauled her, including the renewal of many components. This splendid little engine can often be seen hauling the vintage 'Stately Trains' and also stars as 'Percy' during the Thomas the Tank Engine events.

The climb away from Stoneacre offers the opportunity to see and photograph the locomotives working hard, especially during the peak season when two-train operation requires trains to stop at the loop to allow the footplate crews to exchange tokens.

The whole operation can be witnessed from the grass verge of the A59 road above Holywell Bridge. On a cold December afternoon these Santa Specials have just crossed and with the low winter sun lengthening shadows with every passing minute, excited Bolton Abbey-bound children will be about to meet Santa, those returning to Embsay will be unwrapping their present and mum and dad will be washing down their mince pie with a glass of sherry!

The same operation viewed from a lower perspective much later in the day
with the hillside clinging to the last of the day's light.

Once clear of the loop the line climbs towards Holywell Halt. The little blue engine is about to enter the cutting that marks the final approach to the halt.

Likewise 'Monckton No.1' and its Vintage Train announce their arrival with an equally impressive smoky display.

The train here is the return working of that photographed earlier in the day and included on page 47. The bridge in the background being the vantage point for that particular shot.

The railway also provides for geologically minded people because the cutting immediately to the east of the Halt is designated a Site of Special Scientific Interest as it provides exposures of the lowest beds of the carboniferous limestone visible in the Craven District. By pure coincidence this photograph was taken by Karl who having recently achieved a BSc in Geography/Geology at the University of Manchester will understand what I have just written! (Karl Heath)

As the railway provides the only access to Holywell Halt it is a wonderfully peaceful location and well worth being 'dropped off' at to spend a little time photographing trains as they pass through.

With the vintage coaches from the 'Stately Trains' collection alongside
the platform the location takes on a Victorian air.

Leaving Holywell the line continues to climb towards the summit at Skibeden.

Footbridges are excellent vantage points affording the opportunity to photograph a train as it approaches . . .

. . . then turning for the 'going away' shot. Plus, with the raised vantage point, the surrounding landscape, which would be lost if the photographer was at track level, can be included in the picture. (Karl Heath)

The coach at the rear of this vintage train is a former Lancashire and Yorkshire carriage which was built in 1906 for the company's directors allowing them to travel their system in very comfortable conditions as they inspected the various routes. It had been rebuilt under both the LMS and British Railways but has now been restored to its original condition. The large windows give passengers splendid views of the line's scenery.

Echoes of the past are stirred as a mixed freight train containing a number of stone hoppers passes beneath the edge of the High Skibeden Quarry.

This panoramic view places the railway in the centre of the wonderful Dales scenery with its winding narrow stonewall-bounded lanes, rolling tree-lined hills and undulating fields kept neat and tidy by the grazing sheep.

Opposite:
Passing the same point in December 2007 this double-headed Santa Special
drifts down the gradual descent to Embsay Station.

Another demonstration freight has just received permission to approach the station via the aloft arm of the 'outer home' signal visible mid right in the photograph. In the background is the edge of the giant Haw Bank Quarry which dominates the landscape to the east of the station.

The view from the eastern end of platform 2 on the afternoon of the 2003 Steam Gala as 'Primrose No. 2' arrives back at Embsay. On the coal dock road 'Wheldale' and the visiting '4F' have been coaled and watered in readiness for their next duties.

On the equivalent weekend some nine years earlier 'Wheldale' was again captured between
duties as the railway's then recent acquisition No. 68005 arrived alongside the platform
with a demonstration freight just before the heavens opened.

Branch Line Day 20 September 1992 and the arrival of 'Primrose No. 2' and its train are viewed from the footbridge. On this occasion 'Wheldale' had been rostered for the next departure.

In the summer of 2000 a couple of weekends were spent photographing that season's Vintage Train specials. On 16 July the diminutive 'Annie' was providing the motive power.

Whereas the previous Sunday had seen 'Cranford No. 2' in charge. On both weekends the vintage stock had comprised former Great Eastern Railway Carriage No. 14, here immediately behind the locomotive, which had been built in 1889 and had no doubt hauled VIPs all over the GER. The projecting window denotes that the coach has a guard's compartment. The second carriage, No. 37, was also built by the Great Eastern Railway as a saloon and it is reputed to have been the private saloon of Princess Alice as, during restoration, several internal features not normally associated with third class accommodation were discovered.

A freight train arrives alongside platform 2 already strewn with luggage destined for the lost property office!

Another arrival emerges from the gloom of a recent storm to be welcomed by a shaft
of sunlight. A relief to both the passengers and the photographer!

This passenger service has terminated at Embsay and the locomotive has just been unhooked from the carriages prior to running round to prepare for the next departure to Bolton Abbey.

However, during high season most services from Bolton Abbey will pass through the station without stopping. On these occasions the passengers are treated to an extended trip including the short stretch of line to the run-round loop at Bow Bridge.

From high above the loop the sweep of the Grassington Branch can clearly be determined as it snakes along the contours of the land on its way to Tilcon's Swinden Quarry. Since 1969 the expanded Lime Works at Swinden has been the sole reason for the survival of this section of line.

Whilst the Embsay & Bolton Abbey Steam Railway harbours plans that will see reconnection
of the railway with Skipton, for now Bow Bridge is the western extent of the line.

With the run-round operation almost completed it will not be
long before the train is on the move once again. (Karl Heath)

The railway's Diesel Multiple Unit powers its way along the branch back towards
the station. This vantage point allows a grand overview of Embsay village and the crag above.

Passing the same location in the summer of 2007 is the Llangollen Railway's 0-6-0 ST 'Jessie'.

For the 2006 'Harvest of Steam' this Beyer Peacock 0-4-0 ST locomotive was brought in from the Foxfield Railway to cover for 'Cranford' which had been withdrawn for repairs. Unfortunately it also had problems and saw very limited use. However it certainly looked the part on this cold damp afternoon as it trundled down to Bow Bridge and back with a very short freight train.

In the very early days of preservation the society raised money by giving brake van rides between Embsay and Bow Bridge. It may not be the most luxurious way to travel but if you ever get the opportunity to ride in a guards van I recommend you give it a try.

A busy scene at Embsay captured between showers during the 1994 'Harvest of Steam' weekend. The station buildings at Embsay are in the main those built by the Midland Railway in 1888, although the interiors have been altered to provide passenger facilities. Additional timber buildings have been acquired including a former cabman's shelter from Ilkley Station, and a ticket office from Barmouth Station in mid-Wales. Both these buildings can be seen in one of the photographs on page 66.

In my view, with two ex-industrial tank engines in charge, this photograph
epitomises the Embsay & Bolton Abbey Steam Railway of today.

Whereas with a former LMS tender locomotive providing the motive power,
this scene is more typical of the railway as it was over sixty years ago.

From the outset the railway has held regular events aimed at the family market and for the younger enthusiasts Thomas the Tank Engine Weekends based on the character created by the Reverend W. Awdry were an instant success. Latterly 'Ivor the Engine' created by Oliver Postgate and Peter Fimin, has made the first of what will no doubt become many visits to the line.

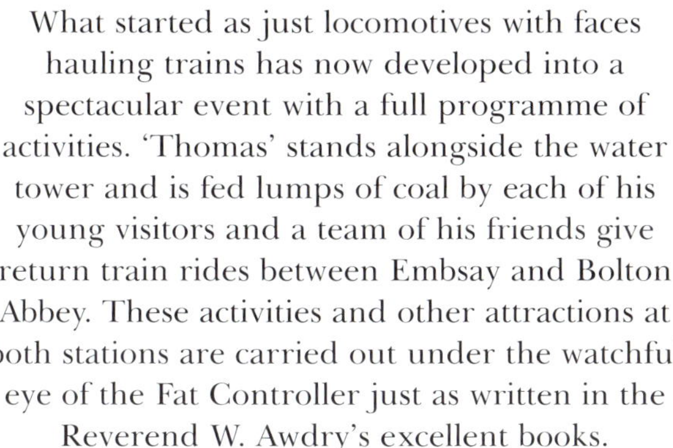

What started as just locomotives with faces hauling trains has now developed into a spectacular event with a full programme of activities. 'Thomas' stands alongside the water tower and is fed lumps of coal by each of his young visitors and a team of his friends give return train rides between Embsay and Bolton Abbey. These activities and other attractions at both stations are carried out under the watchful eye of the Fat Controller just as written in the Reverend W. Awdry's excellent books.

On occasions, again just like in the books, 'Thomas' has been known to be very naughty by going out on the main line pretending to be a big engine!

For many years on the Saturday
nearest to November 5th the
railway held a spectacular Bonfire
and Firework Night, an event
which all my family eagerly looked
forward to. (Karl Heath)

The challenge of photographing steam
locomotives at night is one that I have
always thoroughly enjoyed and
capturing on film the light trails of
exploding fireworks has always made
for stunning images. An event that
provided the opportunity to hone one's
skills at both was not to be missed.

Opposite:
For the duration of the firework display
the train services were suspended and
the footplate crew took the opportunity
to replenish the locomotive's water
tank. On this occasion the light from
the bonfire, which was located near to
the water tower, provided strong
backlighting creating this locomotive
silhouette.

To enable an intensive service to operate, the trains were 'topped and tailed' thus negating the need for locomotives to run round between trains. So one year I watched the display from the western end of the station.

But most years the position opposite the coal dock proved the best vantage point.
In 1993 'Beatrice' provided the foreground interest.

The following year No. 68005 took centre stage.

And in 1998 the Embsay-facing 'Primrose' took pole position.

The pyrotechnics were not the only special effects of these evenings. Here set against the bonfire's golden glow the long exposure has created what appears to be a tornado of steam above the locomotive.

This photograph is very special to me being the first one I had had published in a magazine. It was taken in 1988 and is of the Well Tank locomotive 'Bellerophon' at that year's Bonfire Night event.

From the end of November Santa Specials take centre stage as Santa Claus visits the railway,
travelling on all trains and dispensing gifts to the children as they travel along the line.

The station buildings are festooned
with seasonal decorations and
illuminations.

New Years Day 2008 was very dull and drizzly and not conducive to any satisfactory photography but with the timetable including trains running after dark the resultant damp platforms greatly enhanced the night-time scene.

And the festive lighting around the station provided superb background detail.

One last look back before the final train of the day sets off back to Embsay.